INDO-CHINA

SUMATRAN

SIBERIAN

*To Mommom—for always
being a source of fierceness*

Published by Roaring Brook Press • Roaring Brook Press is a division of Holtzbrinck Publishing Holdings Limited Partnership •
120 Broadway, New York, NY 10271 • mackids.com • Copyright © 2022 by Lily Williams • All rights reserved. • Our books may be
purchased in bulk for promotional, educational, or business use. Please contact your local bookseller or the Macmillan Corporate
and Premium Sales Department at (800) 221-7945 ext. 5442 or by email at MacmillanSpecialMarkets@macmillan.com • Library of
Congress Cataloging-in-Publication Data is available • First edition, 2022 • Book design by Marissa Asuncion • The illustrations in this
book were created digitally in Adobe Photoshop. • Printed in Malaysia by Ruho Corporation Sdn. Bhd. • ISBN 978-1-250-23246-5 •
10 9 8 7 6 5 4 3 2 1

IF TIGERS
DISAPPEARED

Lily Williams

ROARING BROOK PRESS
NEW YORK

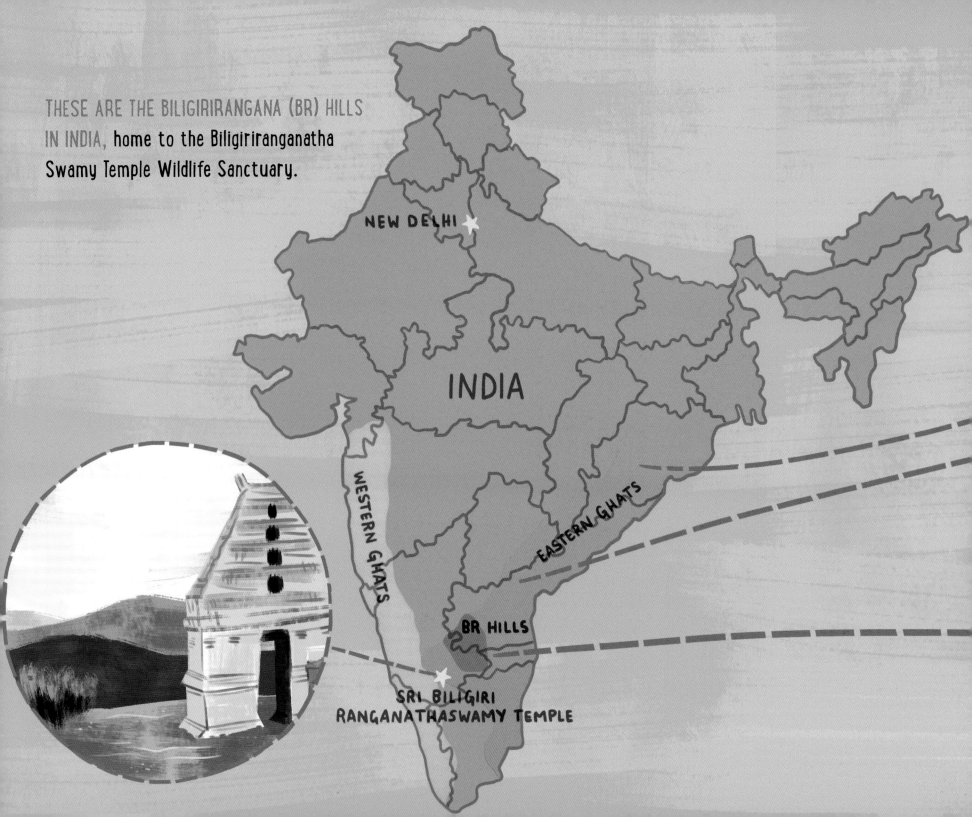

THESE ARE THE BILIGIRIRANGANA (BR) HILLS IN INDIA, home to the Biligiriranganatha Swamy Temple Wildlife Sanctuary.

NEW DELHI ★

INDIA

WESTERN GHATS

EASTERN GHATS

BR HILLS

SRI BILIGIRI RANGANATHASWAMY TEMPLE ★

This area, located in the Eastern Ghats, is a lushly
populated home to animals that
jump,
pounce,
stomp, and . . .

Tiger ancestors can be traced back to Africa more than two million years ago. Over time, they left Africa and moved into Asia, where they slowly evolved into the nine subspecies of tiger, six of which are still alive today.

RUSSIA

MONGOLIA

N. KOREA

JAPAN

CHINA

S. KOREA

AFGHANISTAN

NEPAL

BHUTAN

PAKISTAN

INDIA

LAOS

TAIWAN

BURMA

BANGLADESH

VIETNAM

PHILIPPINES

THAILAND

CAMBODIA

SRI LANKA

MALAYSIA

INDONESIA

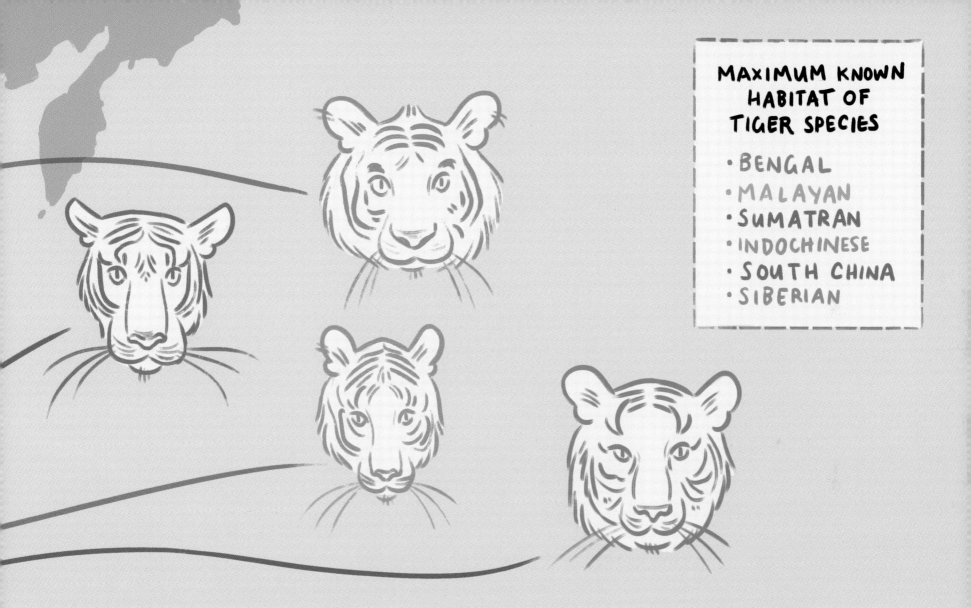

The smallest subspecies of tiger is the Sumatran tiger, which can weigh 250 pounds and grow to between six and eight feet in length, while the biggest tiger in India is the Siberian tiger, which can weigh over 660 pounds and be over ten feet in length! Most of the world's wild tiger population is made up of Bengal tigers, who mainly live in India.

In 1900, there were an estimated one hundred thousand tigers in the wild, but from 1900 to 2000, tiger populations declined by 96 percent. As human populations expand, tigers lose more and more of their natural land. Today, due to habitat loss and poaching, fewer than four thousand tigers remain in the wild.

As apex predators, tigers rule the vast forests, swamps, and mountains they inhabit. A single tiger's territory can be over 25,000 acres of land.

NEW
JERSEY

THE BRONX

MANHATTAN

QUEENS

BROOKLYN

25,000 ACRES
IN NEW YORK

If Bengal tigers disappeared . . .

The populations of sambar, chital, and other large mammals that tigers eat would grow out of control. Large mammals help maintain the landscape by eating, denning, and walking through large areas of forest. With few other apex predators to help control the populations of these large mammals . . .

Their patterns of eating, denning, and walking through the forest would slowly erode waterways and change the landscapes the water runs through. This would affect plant growth patterns, making it impossible for some species of natural flora and fauna to survive.

The combination of these events could completely alter the forest landscape.

If the forest landscape changed . . .

Smaller animals that call the waterways and plants home would quickly die out. Without their usual plants and animals to live off of, insects might be pushed into human areas, searching for new places to reproduce and feed.

If insect populations changed . . .

So would the world as we know it.

This ripple effect, called the trophic cascade, can spill out across the world, affecting all forms of life. What might feel like a threat to a single animal population far away can actually have effects that reach your ecosystem as well.

While humans have taken over a lot of the natural land that tigers inhabit, much hope lies with people and what we can do to help tigers.

Many indigenous communities who worship and help protect tigers believe that tigers and people can coexist in harmony. However, some local people have had to resettle due to tiger wildlife sanctuaries being established on their land. The indigenous people are the best at maintaining their land and conserving it, and relocating people from their ancestral homes throws off the balance in these locations.

The best thing you can do to help save tigers is to learn how important they are to their ecosystems and to share this information, because if we roar loud enough for them . . .

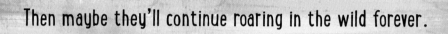

Then maybe they'll continue roaring in the wild forever.

GLOSSARY

BIODIVERSITY: the variety of living organisms in a specific area.

CHITAL: a spotted deer that is native to India.

DEFORESTATION: the human-backed clearing or cutting down of a forest from its land to use the land for other things.

DENNING: a place where a wild animal lives and how it makes its home there.

ECOSYSTEM: the complicated biological system of connected living and nonliving organisms and their physical environment.

FAUNA: the animal life of a specific region or geologic time.

FLORA: the plant life of a specific region or geologic time.

ICONOGRAPHY: images or symbols related to a subject, which are often religious in nature.

INDIGENOUS: native to a specific place.

KEYSTONE SPECIES: a species that shapes its ecosystem such that the ecosystem would be far different without that species.

LANDSCAPE: all aspects of a place (land), generally referring to the visual details.

ORGANISM: a life form (a plant, animal, or single-celled organism).

RESETTLE: to move from one place to live in a different and new place.

SAMBAR: a large deer native to South Asia.

TEMPLE: a building for worshipping a god, gods, or other aspects of a religion.

TERRITORY: an area belonging to an entity (defined by animal, people, plant life, or government).

WILDLIFE SANCTUARY: a place where animals are brought to live so they can be protected.

TIGERS ARE IN TROUBLE

Tiger populations are in trouble. Humans have caused tiger populations to decline by over 96 percent from 1900 to 2000 through poaching, illegal wildlife trade, and other activities fueled by greed and money.

From early depictions of tigers in historical artwork to religious practices around the world featuring tiger imagery and iconography, tigers have been important to many communities and cultures through time. While not as celebrated as they once were, tigers are still worshipped by many indigenous communities to this day. The indigenous people featured in *If Tigers Disappeared* are the Soliga people, who live in the Biligirirangana Hills and areas around southern Karnataka in India. The belief that the indigenous people can help protect the animals that live in their ancestral land is one that should be respected. However, that belief is frequently challenged (often in the name of protecting animals) by governments and non-native people across the world. The Soliga people face such displacement in the BR Hills of India as the Indian government pushes to move indigenous people from their lands to make tiger reserves.

We cannot talk about conservation, biodiversity, and saving endangered species without discussing the indigenous communities who have protected and worked their lands for centuries in sustainable and nature-honoring ways. When we discuss how to help save tigers and protect the biodiversity that tigers help maintain, it is wise to look to the people who have lived with these creatures and worshipped them throughout history. When we listen to indigenous communities, we can often learn the best ways to respect endangered species and the land they protect.

HOW YOU CAN HELP SAVE TIGERS

While not everyone can do everything, here are many ways you can help save tigers.

- Roar for tigers like they roar for you! Stand up and spread the word about how important tigers are to our planet by using your skills . . . maybe you dance, draw, sing, or do math? Help save tigers in your unique way!
- Adopt a tiger online! Many environmental organizations allow you to symbolically adopt a tiger to help their efforts protecting tigers.
- Make sure the zoo or wildlife sanctuary you visit has acquired their tigers ethically. When animals are illegally acquired, it means they are kidnapped from their homes, often to be put on display for money from visitors who want to interact with the large cats. Responsible zoos and wildlife sanctuaries won't let visitors touch their large cats.
- When you travel (across the country and the world), leave nature the way you found it and take only memories.
- Be mindful of your purchases and buy things that have clear labeling showing they were taken or created with our planet's health in mind. Don't purchase tiger parts, goods, or medicines, and be mindful of paper and wood sources.
- With the aid of an adult, sign petitions to help save tigers. Write to your government representatives to tell them to prevent deforestation and strengthen animal import laws. Also, tell the adults in your life to vote for representatives who will do these things!

AUTHOR'S NOTE

The information in this book is a simplified description of a complicated process.
To learn more, start with the bibliography listed on the next page.

The If . . . Disappeared series was born out of a love for one special animal: sharks. This love I have for sharks transformed into a desire to save them when I realized I had a voice and could roar, like tigers. Using my art and my words to inspire, I could help save sharks through teaching others about why they're so important to our world in *If Sharks Disappeared. If Tigers Disappeared* is the fifth installment of the If . . . Disappeared series. Every book allows me to look across the globe to learn about different species of animals and their importance to our planet.

While I cannot travel physically to do work on the If . . . Disappeared books, I get to meet amazing people and learn from them directly or through their work. I practice writing and rewriting, constantly fact-checking my book against the work of these experts. Something I've learned from all the people who are helping animals and our planet is how important each of our voices is. Just on this project alone, I was lucky enough to learn from the work of scientists, photographers, filmmakers, journalists, data collectors, and government officials. All these people are working to save tigers and using their unique skill sets to accomplish this together. The different skills people have are the ways they roar, like tigers, for our world. For me, I can only hope to add to their work through my skills, which are writing and drawing. Tigers have taught me that if there's something wonderful we have, it's our ability to roar . . . and when we roar together, we can make a difference. How do you roar?

ACKNOWLEDGMENTS

This book would not exist without the following people who aided in my research and exploration: my family—who encouraged me to roar; Minju Chang of BookStop Literary Agency, who helps me pounce; Emily Feinberg of Roaring Brook Press, who allowed me to look across the globe; the art direction team that has taken these books to the next level over the years; the publicity and school and library teams, who deserve a round of a-paws; my uncle Michael Benanav, who let me practice illustrating books using his—and helped take me on a world adventure with this one; the fierce Lucrecia Aguilar, for telling me tales about tigers; and *you*, for listening, reading, and helping to spread the word. Let's stand tall for tigers together!

BIBLIOGRAPHY

Benanav, Michael. "Can Tribes and Tigers Coexist in India's Nature Reserves?" *Sierra.* Sierra Club, June 15, 2017. Web. 2020.

Benanav, Michael. *Traditional Cultures Project.* Traditional Cultures Project. Web 2020

"Email exchange about tigers with Lucrecia Aguilar." Email interview. 2020.

"Email with Michael Benanav." Email interview. 2020.

"Frequently Asked Questions—Tiger." *World Wildlife Fund India.* World Wildlife Fund. Web. 2020.

Kumara, Honnavalli N. *Fig 1.* Digital image. *ResearchGate.* 1999. Web. February 25, 2021.

Patel, Krunal. "Tiger Census 2018 Report—Tiger Population in India 2019." *Big Cats India.* Big Cats India, February 8, 2018. Web. 2020.

Platt, John R. "6 Reasons We Should Still Worry About Tigers." *Scientific American.* April 14, 2016. Web. 2020.

"Tiger Reports." *Wildlife Institute of India.* Government of India, October 1, 2020. Web. 2020.

"Tigers 101 | National Geographic." youtube.com. *National Geographic,* February 8, 2019. Web. 2020.

Vince, Gaia. "Tigers: Can We Afford to Save Them?" *BBC*, March 19, 2012. Web. 2020.

"What Would Be the Impact if the Tiger Disappeared?" *Awely*, November 20, 2015. Web. 2020.

Winter, Steve, and Sharon Guynup. *Tigers Forever: Saving the World's Most Endangered Big Cat.* Washington, DC: National Geographic Society, 2013. Print.

BENGAL

MALAYAN

SOUTH CHINA